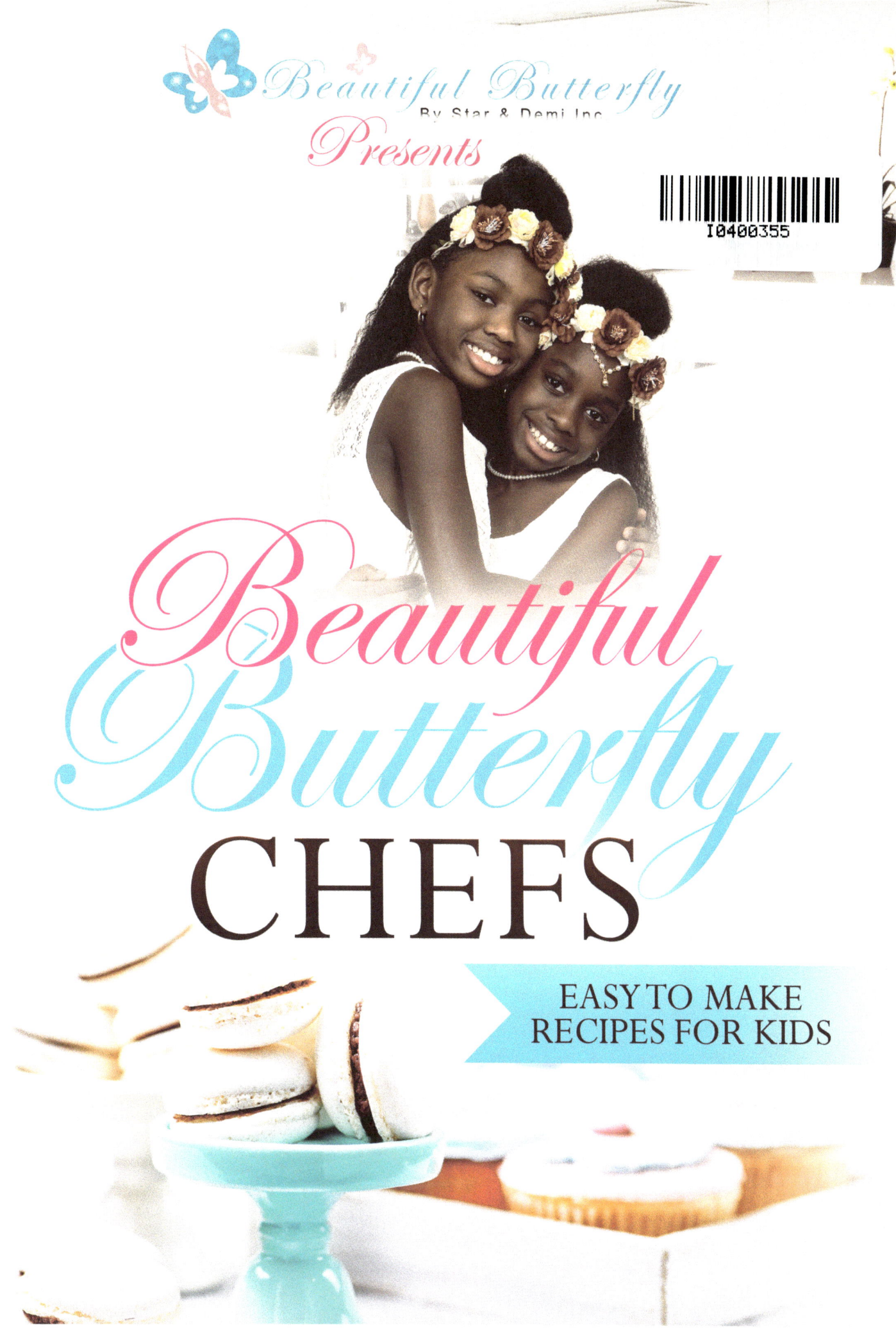

Beautiful Butterfly Chefs: Easy to Make recipes for kids

Copyright © 2019 by Star Devyne Harris & Demi Harris

All rights reserved. This book or any portion thereof may not be reproduced or used in any manner whatsoever without the express written permission of the publisher except for the use of brief quotations in a book review.

Printed in the United States of America

First Printing

A2Z Books Publishing
Lithonia, GA 30058

www.A2ZBooksPublishing.net

Manufactured in the United States of America

A2Z Books Publishing has allowed this work to remain exactly as the author intended, verbatim.

Fluffy Waffles with Fruits 2

French Toasts 3

Breakfast Corndog 4

Banana Nut Pancakes 5

Chicken Fingers 6

Gourmet Hot Dogs with Aioli Sauce 7

Ham & Grilled Cheese 8

Peanut Butter & Jelly Rolls 9

Burger Sliders 10

Chicken Ramen 11

Macaroni & Cheese 12

Grilled Chicken Skewers 13

Macaroons 14

Mini Cupcakes 15

Brownies 16

Rice Crispy Treats 17

Fruit Salad 18

Veggie Dipper 19

Fruit Parfaits 20

Banana Nut Muffins 21

Fresh Fruit Smoothie 22

Fresh Lemonade 23

Skittles Soda 24

Strawberry Milk Shake 25

Fluffy Waffles with Fruits

Prep Time: 15 minutes
Cooking Time: 5 minutes
Servings: 4

Ingredients:

- 1 ½ cup flour
- ½ cup cornstarch
- 2 eggs, room temperature
- 1 teaspoon baking powder
- ½ teaspoon baking soda
- ½ cup skim milk
- 5 tablespoons vegetable oil
- 2 teaspoons vanilla extract
- 2 tablespoons sugar
- ½ cup club soda
- ½ teaspoon salt
- 1 cup sliced bananas
- 1 cup sliced strawberries
- 1 cup sliced peaches
- Whipped cream, for serving

Instructions:

1. Separate egg whites and egg yolks.
2. In a big mixing bowl mix together flour, cornstarch, baking powder, baking soda and salt. You can use a fork or hand mixer.
3. Take a separate bowl and mix egg yolks, milk, oil and vanilla there. Mix well, until combined.
4. Use a hand mixer and beat egg whites until you see soft peaks formed. Slowly add sugar to the egg whites and continue mixing for 1-2 minutes.
5. Take a big mixing bowl with dry ingredients and add the mixture with egg yolks, use a mixer to combine everything. Add club soda, slowly add egg whites mixture and whisk well.
6. Preheat the waffle maker. Pour the waffle batter to the waffle maker and cook until brown.
7. Transfer cooked waffles to a plate. Top with whipped cream and sliced fruits. Enjoy!

French Toasts

Prep Time: 5 minutes
Cooking Time: 5 minutes
Servings: 4

Ingredients:
- 4 slices toast bread
- 1 egg
- ¼ cup milk
- ½ teaspoon cinnamon
- 1 teaspoon vanilla extract
- 2 sticks unsalted butter
- 1 cup sliced strawberries

Instructions:
1. In a shallow plate beat egg, vanilla extract and cinnamon; use a fork. Beat for about 1 minute until mixed.
2. Place a non-stick frying pan over medium heat and add 1 stick butter. Wait till butter melts.
3. Dip the bread slices in egg mixture from both sides and place on the skillet. Cook for 2-3 minutes, flip over and cook for 2 minutes on another side.
4. Serve topped with butter and strawberries. Enjoy!

Breakfast Corndog

Prep Time: 15 minutes
Cooking Time: 15 minutes
Servings: 4

Ingredients:

- 8 breakfast sausage links
- ½ cup corn meal
- 1 ½ cups flour
- 1 cup buttermilk
- 1 teaspoon sugar
- ½ teaspoon baking powder
- ¼ teaspoon baking soda
- ¼ cup cornstarch
- 4 cups oil
- Bamboo skewers

Instructions:

1. Place a non-stick frying pan over medium heat and add 1-2 tablespoons oil. Place sausages on the pan and cook for 4-5 minutes until cooked from all sides. Turn off heat and transfer sausages to a plate, cut them in half.
2. In a mixing bowl mix corn meal, flour, sugar, baking soda and baking powder. Add buttermilk and whisk well to combine; you can use a fork or a mixer.
3. Add all 4 cups oil to a deep pan and preheat over medium heat.
4. Insert a bamboo skewer into each sausage. Dip each sausage in cornstarch first, then in corn meal batter. Make sure they are coated well.
5. Carefully drop each sausage into oil and cook for about 1-2 minutes until golden. Use tongs to turn them and to remove from oil.
6. Serve with the syrup of your choice. Enjoy!

Banana Nut Pancakes

Prep Time: 5 minutes
Cooking Time: 5 minutes
Servings: 8

Ingredients:

- 1 cup flour
- 1 egg
- 1 cup milk
- 2 teaspoons sugar
- 1 teaspoon baking powder
- 2 tablespoons oil
- ¼ teaspoon salt
- ½ teaspoon vanilla extract
- 1 banana
- ½ cup crushed walnuts

Instructions:

1. Using a fork mash banana in a plate.
2. In a big mixing bowl combine flour, baking powder, sugar and salt; mix well.
3. Take a separate bowl and whisk milk, egg, oil and vanilla extract, mix until combined.
4. Slowly add egg and milk mixture to the flour mixture and use a mixer to combine ingredients. Mix until all chunks are gone.
5. Add walnuts and mashed banana to the batter, mix well until all ingredients are combined.
6. Place a non-stick frying pan over medium heat and add oil. Wait until it gets hot and pour about ¼ cup batter on the pan. Cook for 2-3 minutes, flip and cook for 2 more minutes. Repeat until all batter is gone. Enjoy!

Chicken Fingers

Prep Time: 15 minutes
Cooking Time: 40 minutes
Servings: 4

Ingredients:
- 1 pound skinless chicken breasts, sliced into strips OR 1 pound chicken tenders
- 1 ½ cup flour
- 1 egg
- 2 tablespoons water
- ½ teaspoon salt
- ¼ teaspoon black pepper
- ½ cup oil

Instructions:
1. In a medium bowl mix flour, salt and pepper.
2. In a separate bowl beat and egg with water.
3. Add oil to the non-stick deep frying pan and preheat over medium heat.
4. Take one chicken strip and dip it into the egg mixture first and then into flour. Add to the pan.
5. Cook for 7-8 minutes until brown. Turn and cook for another 5 minutes. Repeat for the rest of chicken strips.
6. Transfer cooked strips to a plate lined with a paper towel and enjoy!

Gourmet Hot Dogs with Aioli Sauce

Prep Time: 10 minutes
Cooking Time: 25 minutes
Servings: 4

Ingredients:

- 1 package beef franks
- 6 hot dog buns
- 6 Cheddar cheese slices
- 6 lettuce leaves
- 1 tomato, chopped
- 1 red onion, chopped

For Aioli Sauce:

- ½ cup mayonnaise
- 2 garlic cloves, mashed
- 1 tablespoon lemon juice
- 2 tablespoons olive oil
- ¼ teaspoon salt
- ¼ teaspoon black pepper

Instructions:

1. Preheat oven to 400F. Line a baking tray with parchment paper. Place beef flanks on the tray and bake for 15 minutes.
2. Mix mayonnaise, garlic, salt and black pepper in a small bowl. Add lemon juice and oil and mix well.
3. Place hot dog buns on a big serving plate. Place one lettuce leave on each bun, add Cheddar cheese slices on top.
4. Insert one beef flank into each bun, top with tomato and onion and drizzle with cooked sauce. Preserve some sauce for dipping. Enjoy!

Ham & Grilled Cheese

Prep Time: 5 minutes
Cooking Time: 6 minutes
Servings: 2

Ingredients:
- 4 slices toast bread
- 4 slices Cheddar cheese
- 2 slices ham
- 2 tablespoons butter, softened
- 1 teaspoon mustard (optional)

Instructions:
1. Spread mustard on 2 slices of bread. For each sandwich, lay one slice cheese on one slice, top with ham, cheese again and bread.
2. Heat a non-stick frying pan over medium heat and add butter. Place sandwiches on the pan and cook for 2-3 minutes until brown. Turn and cook for 2 more minutes on other side.
3. Transfer to a plate and enjoy!

Peanut Butter & Jelly Rolls

Prep Time: 10 minutes
Cooking Time: 2 minutes + chilling
Servings: 4

Ingredients:

- 4 flour tortillas
- 4 tablespoons Peanut Butter
- ½ cup Strawberry Jelly
- 1 package (3 oz) cream cheese, softened

Instructions:

1. Mix jelly and cream cheese in a bowl, whisk with a mixer.
2. Spread peanut butter on each tortilla, top with jelly cream mixture.
3. Carefully roll up tortillas and wrap each in plastic wrap. Refrigerate for at least 2-4 hours or overnight. Slice and serve!

Burger Sliders

Prep Time: 10 minutes
Cooking Time: 20 minutes
Servings: 12

Ingredients:

- 12 Hawaiian Rolls
- 1 onion, chopped
- 1 lb ground beef
- 6 slices Cheddar or American Cheese
- 24 pickle slices
- 2 tablespoons butter, melted
- 1 tablespoon oil
- ¼ teaspoon salt
- ¼ teaspoon black pepper
- Ketchup
- Mustard

Instructions:

1. Preheat oil in a skillet over medium heat. Add onion and cook for 2-3 minutes. Add ground beef, season with salt and pepper. Cook until beef is no longer pink, breaking the meat while cooking.
2. Preheat oven to 350F. Line an 11x15 baking dish with parchment paper or foil. Coat with cooking spray.
3. Slice the rolls in half and put the bottom part into the baking dish. Spread ketchup and mustard on each roll. Top with cooked beef and onion, add cheese slices and 2 pickles on each roll.
4. Top with the second half of rolls. Brush with melted butter and place into the oven. Cover with aluminum foil and bake for 20 minutes. Enjoy!

Chicken Ramen

Prep Time: 10 minutes
Cooking Time: 30 minutes
Servings: 4

Ingredients:

- 1 onion, diced
- 1 cup Bok Choy Asian cabbage, chopped
- 2 cups cooked shredded chicken
- 1 package (15-16 oz) ramen noodles, cooked according to package instructions
- 6 garlic cloves, diced
- 1-inch fresh ginger root piece, grated
- 6 cups chicken broth
- 1 tablespoon chili garlic sauce
- ¼ cup soy sauce
- 1 tablespoon oil
- 2 green onions, chopped, for serving
- 1 tablespoon fresh cilantro, chopped, for serving
- Salt, pepper, to taste

Instructions:

1. Preheat oil in a skillet over medium heat. Add onion and cook for 5-6 minutes. Add garlic and ginger. Cook for 1 more minute.
2. Add chicken broth, chili garlic sauce and soy sauce. Cook for 20-25 minutes over medium heat.
3. After 20-25 minutes add chicken and Bok Choy. Add salt and pepper to taste.
4. Divide noodles among plates and pour soup on top. Serve!

Macaroni & Cheese

Prep Time: 15 minutes
Cooking Time: 40 minutes
Servings: 4

Ingredients:

- 3 cups elbow macaroni
- 1 onion, chopped
- ½ cup butter
- ½ cup flour
- 4 cups milk
- 1 ½ cups Cheddar cheese, grated
- ½ cup Parmesan cheese, grated
- 1 cup Colby Jack cheese, grated
- ½ cup Monterey Jack cheese, diced
- 1 teaspoon sea salt
- ¼ teaspoon black pepper

Instructions:

1. Fill a medium sauce pan with water and bring to a boil. Add salt and macaroni. Mix with a spoon and cook for 7-8 minutes. Drain and set aside.
2. Melt butter in a medium sized pot over medium heat, add onion and cook for 2-3 minutes, until soften.
3. Add flour and cook for 2-3 more minutes, stirring constantly.
4. Add milk, whisk constantly. Bring the mixture to a boil and reduce the heat to low. Add all the cheeses. Stir and cook until cheeses melt.
5. Pour the mixture over cooked macaroni, stir well to coat and serve!

Grilled Chicken Skewers

Prep Time: 10 minutes
Cooking Time: 10 minutes
Servings: 4

Ingredients:

- 4 chicken breasts, cut into cubes
- 1 red onion, quartered
- 1 bell pepper, cut into chunks
- ½ tablespoon brown sugar
- ½ teaspoon garlic powder
- ½ teaspoon smoked paprika
- 1/8 teaspoon cayenne pepper
- 3 tablespoons oil
- 1 teaspoon salt
- Skewers

Instructions:

1. Preheat the grill to high heat.
2. Add chicken cubes, sugar, garlic powder, smoked paprika, cayenne pepper, oil and salt to a ziplock bag and shake to coat the chicken.
3. Take a skewer, thread a chicken cube onto skewer following by onion and bell pepper. Repeat until the skewer is filled. Repeat for the rest of skewers.
4. Place the skewers on the grill and cook for 3-4 minutes per side, in total for 10-15 minutes.
5. Transfer to a plate and enjoy!

Macaroons

Prep Time: 10 minutes
Cooking Time: 16 minutes
Servings: 12

Ingredients:

- 2 egg whites, from 2 eggs
- ¾ cup powdered sugar + 2/3 cup powdered sugar
- ¼ cup fine sugar
- ¾ cup almond flour
- 2/3 cup unsalted butter, softened
- 2 teaspoons cocoa powder

Instructions:
1. Preheat the oven to 300F.
2. In a medium bowl mix ¾ cup powdered sugar and almond flour.
3. In a separate bowl whisk egg whites and salt until you see soft peaks, use hand mixer. Add fine sugar slowly and keep whisking until the mixture is very thick.
4. Carefully add almond flour mixture to the egg whites mixture and whisk to combine.
5. Prepare a piping bag with a 1/3-inch nozzle, fill it with macaroon mixture.
6. Line a baking sheet with parchment paper. Pipe small blobs of macaroon batter on the tray and leave to dry for 20 minutes.
7. Bake for 7-8 minutes, open the oven door to release some steam and cook for another 708 minutes.
8. Now it's time to make the filling. Beat the butter in a bowl using mixer. Slowly add 2/3 cup powdered sugar and cocoa and whisk again. You can add different flavorings at this stage.
9. Take the macaroons out of the oven, spread the filling on each macaroon half and sandwich halves together. Refrigerate macaroons for at least 4 hours and enjoy!

Mini Cupcakes

Prep Time: 30 minutes
Cooking Time: 12 minutes
Servings: 24

Ingredients:

- 1 ½ cups all-purpose flour
- 2 eggs , room temperature
- ¼ cup cornstarch
- 1 cup granulated sugar
- ½ teaspoon baking soda
- ½ teaspoon baking powder
- ¼ teaspoon salt
- ½ cup unsalted butter, softened
- 2 teaspoons vanilla extract
- 3 tablespoons sour cream
- ½ cup milk , room temperature

For Chocolate Buttercream:
- 2 oz chocolate bar
- 2/3 cup unsalted butter, softened
- 1 cup powdered sugar
- 2 tablespoons milk

Instructions:

1. Preheat the oven to 350F. Line mini muffin pans with muffin paper.
2. In a big bowl mix flour, cornstarch, baking soda, baking powder and salt.
3. In a separate bowl whisk together ½ cup butter and granulated sugar, beat until fluffy.
4. Add eggs and vanilla, keep mixing. Add sour cream and mix until combined. Use a spatula to scrape down bowl sides.
5. Slowly add flour mixture and mix with the mixer on low speed. Add milk, keep mixing.
6. Fill each muffin pan with batter (to ¾ full) and bake for 11-12 minutes.
7. Meanwhile cook the buttercream. Melt chocolate in the microwave. In a bowl mix chocolate, 2/3 cup butter, powdered sugar and 2 tablespoons milk. Transfer the mixture to a pastry bag fitted with a star nozzle and top each cupcake. Enjoy!

Brownies

Prep Time: 10 minutes
Cooking Time: 30 minutes
Servings: 12

Ingredients:
- ¾ cup flour
- 1 ½ cups sugar
- 3 eggs
- 1/3 cup + 2 ½ tablespoons cocoa powder
- ¾ cup oil
- 1 ½ teaspoon vanilla extract
- ¼ teaspoon + 1/8 teaspoon baking powder
- ¼ teaspoon salt

Instructions:
1. Preheat the oven to 350F. Line a square baking pan with parchment paper.
2. Mix sugar, vanilla and oil in a bowl. Add eggs and mix until all the ingredients are combined.
3. In a separate bowl mix flour, cocoa powder, salt and baking powder.
4. Slowly add egg mixture to the flour mixture and whisk until combined, with a mixer.
5. Pour the batter into a baking pan and bake for 25-30 minutes.
6. Take out from the oven and let rest for 5-10 minutes. Cut into squares and enjoy!

Rice Crispy Treats

Prep Time: 5 minutes
Cooking Time: 5 minutes
Servings: 12

Ingredients:
- 6 tablespoons unsalted butter
- 6 cups mini marshmallows
- 6 cups Rice Krispies

Instructions:
1. Add butter to a medium pan and melt it over medium heat. Add marshmallows, stir well until they melt completely. Turn off the heat.
2. Add Rice Krispies and stir well to coat all the cereals.
3. Prepare a 9x11 inches pan and transfer the Krispies mixture to the pan, spread on the bottom and press down into the pan.
4. Allow to cool, cut into squares and enjoy!

Fruit Salad

Prep Time: 15 minutes
Cooking Time: 1 minute
Servings: 8

Ingredients:

- 2 cups fresh strawberries, quartered
- 3 kiwis, peeled and sliced
- 1 orange, peeled and cubed
- 1 mango, peeled and chopped
- 2 apples, shredded
- ¾ cup blueberries
- ¾ cup raspberries
- ¼ cup honey
- ¼ cup orange juice, freshly squeezed
- 1 lemon, zested

Instructions:

1. In a small bowl mix honey, orange juice and lemon zest.
2. In a big salad bowl mix all the fruits and berries. Pour honey dressing on top and toss well to coat. Enjoy!

Veggie Dipper

Prep Time: 20 minutes
Cooking Time: 2 minutes + chilling
Servings: 8

Ingredients:
- 1 cup mayonnaise
- 1 cup sour cream
- ¼ cup buttermilk
- 1 teaspoon salt
- 1 teaspoon Italian seasoning
- 1 teaspoon garlic powder
- ¼ teaspoon black pepper
- Vegetables: carrots, celery, cucumbers, bell peppers, cut into sticks

Instructions:
1. In a medium bowl mix mayonnaise, sour cream, buttermilk, salt, Italian seasoning, garlic powder and black pepper. Cover and refrigerate for at least 1 hour.
2. Serve the dip with veggies. Enjoy!

Fruit Parfaits

Prep Time: 5 minutes
Cooking Time: 5 minutes + chilling
Servings: 2

Ingredients:
- 1 cup vanilla yogurt
- ½ cup fresh chopped strawberries
- ½ cup chopped kiwi
- 1 banana, sliced
- ½ cup granola

Instructions:
1. Prepare glasses for parfaits. Layer 1 tablespoon yogurt into the bottom of each glass. Top with part of fruits and granola, add more yogurt.
2. Repeat layers. Refrigerate for at least 1 hour and enjoy!

Banana Nut Muffins

Prep Time: 10 minutes
Cooking Time: 25 minutes
Servings: 12

Ingredients:
- 5 bananas
- 1 egg
- 1 cup walnuts, chopped
- 1 ½ cup flour
- 1 teaspoon vanilla extract
- 1 teaspoon baking soda
- ½ teaspoon ground cinnamon
- ½ tablespoon oil or cooking spray
- A pinch of salt

Instructions:
1. Preheat the oven to 350F. Line muffin pans with muffin paper and grease with oil or cooking spray.
2. Mash bananas with a fork in a medium bowl. Add egg and vanilla extract, mix well to combine.
3. In a separate bowl mix flour, baking soda, cinnamon and salt.
4. Add flour mix to the egg banana mixture and use mixer to combine everything.
5. Add walnuts and stir well to incorporate nuts. Pour batter into the muffin pans.
6. Bake for 20-25 minutes. Allow to cool and enjoy!

Fresh Fruit Smoothie

Prep Time: 10 minutes
Cooking Time: 5 minutes
Servings: 2

Ingredients:
- 1 cup strawberries, stemmed
- ½ cup pineapple chunks
- ½ banana
- ½ cup milk
- ½ cup grape juice
- ½ lemon, juiced
- Handful seedless small grapes

Instructions:
1. Add all ingredients to the blender.
2. Process until smooth. Add ice cubes if you want. Enjoy!

Fresh Lemonade

Prep Time: 10 minutes
Cooking Time: 5 minutes
Servings: 6

Ingredients:
- 1 cup freshly squeezed lemon juice
- 4 cups water
- 1 cup white sugar

Instructions:
1. Add 1 cup water and sugar to a saucepan and heat over medium heat. Bring to a boil and cook stirring until sugar dissolves. Remove from heat.
2. Add lemon juice to a serving pitcher. Add sugar and water mixture and the rest of water (3 cups).
3. Refrigerate for 30-40 minutes. Serve with sliced lemon.

Skittles Soda

Prep Time: 5 minutes
Cooking Time: 5 minutes
Servings: 4

Ingredients:
- 1-2 packages Skittles
- 4 cups Sprite soda

Instructions:
1. Separate Skittles candies into different colors. Place each color into one glass.
2. Pour soda into each glass and mix well.
3. Serve immediately. Enjoy!

Strawberry Milk Shake

Prep Time: 10 minutes
Cooking Time: 10 minutes
Servings: 4

Ingredients:
- ½ lb fresh strawberries, stemmed
- 1 cup milk
- 2 cups vanilla ice cream
- ½ teaspoon vanilla extract

Instructions:
1. Add half of strawberries, vanilla extract, 1 cup ice cream and 2 tablespoons milk to a blender. Process until smooth.
2. Divide shake among glasses. Add the rest of ingredients to the blender and process. Pour into glasses and enjoy!

Interested in Writing and or Publishing a BOOK???

Contact : Dr. Synovia www.A2ZBooksPublishing.net

www.ingramcontent.com/pod-product-compliance
Lightning Source LLC
Chambersburg PA
CBHW051351110526
44591CB00025B/2973